BOOKWORMS

Migrating Animals

Butterflies

B.J. Best

Cavendish Square
New York

Published in 2017 by Cavendish Square Publishing, LLC
243 5th Avenue, Suite 136, New York, NY 10016

First Edition

Website: cavendishsq.com

Library of Congress Cataloging-in-Publication Data

Names: Best, B. J., 1976- author.
Title: Butterflies / B.J. Best.
Description: New York : Cavendish Square Publishing, [2017] | Series: Migrating animals | Includes index.
Identifiers: LCCN 2016024590 (print) | LCCN 2016026823 (ebook) | ISBN 9781502620903 (pbk.) | ISBN 9781502620910 (6 pack) | ISBN 9781502620927 (library bound) | ISBN 9781502620934 (E-book)
Subjects: LCSH: Monarch butterfly--Migration--Juvenile literature. | Butterflies--Juvenile literature.
Classification: LCC QL561.D3 B47 2017 (print) | LCC QL561.D3 (ebook) | DDC 595.78/9--dc23
LC record available at https://lccn.loc.gov/2016024590

Editorial Director: David McNamara
Copy Editor: Nathan Heidelberger
Associate Art Director: Amy Greenan
Designer: Alan Sliwinski
Production Assistant: Karol Szymczuk
Photo Research: J8 Media

The photographs in this book are used by permission and through the courtesy of: Cover Sean Xu/Shutterstock; p. 5 pernsanitfoto/Shutterstock; p. 7 Toshiaki Ono/amanaimagesRF/Thinkstock; p. 9 Roger Lecuyer/Istock; p. 11 Richard Ellis/Getty Images News/Getty Images; p. 13 Sean Crane/Minden Pictures/Getty Images; p. 15 Gary W. Carter/Getty Images Entertainment/Getty Images; p. 17 Amith Nag Photography/Getty Images Entertainment/Getty Images; p. 19 Joel Sartore/Getty Images Entertainment/Getty Images; p. 21 OGphoto/Getty Images Entertainment/Getty Images.

Printed in the United States of America

Contents

Butterflies are **insects**.

They have colorful wings.

Some butterflies **migrate**.

They fly very far from one place to another.

The **monarch** is a butterfly.

It flies over 2,000 miles
(3,200 kilometers)!

Monarchs spend summer in the United States and Canada.

They fly to **Mexico** for the winter.

It is warm and safe in Mexico.

Monarchs leave Mexico on the first day of spring.

They fly north.

They look for **milkweed** to eat.

In the fall, milkweed plants start to die.

It becomes cold.

The monarchs can't stay.

New monarchs fly south on the first day of fall.

They use the sun to know where they are going.

Many other butterflies migrate.

They migrate so they always live in a place that's right for them.

New Words

insects (IN-sekts) Bugs.

Mexico (MEK-sih-ko) The country south of the United States.

migrate (MY-grate) To travel far to live in a new place.

milkweed (MILK-weed) A plant that has a white juice that looks like milk.

monarch (MAH-nark) A butterfly with orange and black wings.

Index

About the Author

B.J. Best lives in Wisconsin with his wife and son. He has written several other books for children. He sees monarch butterflies in his garden.

About BOOKWORMS

Bookworms help independent readers gain reading confidence through high-frequency words, simple sentences, and strong picture/text support. Each book explores a concept that helps children relate what they read to the world they live in.